The Narcissist As Parent

Drew Brett

Drew Brett

The Narcissist As Parent
Copyright © 2014 by Drew Brett
First Printing, 2014

In Dedication

I dedicate this not only to the many friends, supporters, and mental health professionals that have helped me through the years, but to the unknown and nameless victims of domestic abuse and violence. Too often, victims, especially child victims, suffer in complete silence and that doesn't have to be the case.

Although I understand that I am far from the only one with a story such as this, it is my hope that, by sharing this story, that it may lend help to others. Maybe it will help someone identify someone close to them that is struggling quietly in a domestic abuse environment. Or maybe a young woman will read this story and see some similarities in her significant other and find the courage to walk away before children become a part of the relationship.

Domestic abuse and violence forces needless and sometimes irreversible suffering and damage on its victims, namely children, and that shouldn't be the type of environment that anyone is forced to be a part of. Part of my healing process is accepting and understanding that I was put here for a reason, if for no other reason than to tell the story. It is my story, one that no one else can put down in words.

With that, I hope that those who have suffered greatly can see that there can be joy and real peace in the journey to healing through self-introspection, rediscovery, and personal growth. It is possible to rebuild a life torn apart by deep emotional and psychological traumas. It can't be done all at once and I have accepted that as part of my journey towards leading a more fulfilling, happy, peaceful life filled with positive moments. It is never too late to make better memories.

By sharing this personal story, if it helps one person or one family remove themselves from a toxic and dangerous situation, then it makes it worth it. It is also my hope that by sharing this story that people will pay more attention to those around them. I challenge everyone to learn and understand the signs of narcissistic abuse patterns in families and reach out to those in need, especially children who may have no one to turn to. For a child being abused and neglected in this manner, it is a lonely life, one filled with despair and sadness. If everyone does their part and pays attention to those around them, it doesn't have to be like that.

The Narcissist As Parent

Chapter 1 - Early Family Life

My earliest memories of my life were of a family in a constant state of emotional and psychological chaos and turmoil. Feelings of terror and fear were constant. We never knew when or why we might see another episode of rage and abuse. The unpredictable nature of it left my family in an endless state of fear. Oftentimes, fear filled my mind as I tried to find a safe place to hide from that scary presence in my home.

Unfortunately, there were no safe hiding places.

For a small child, home wasn't a place to feel safe, to feel peace or joy.

The fear and terror was always there, an absolute in my life, because no one could make it go away.

That presence, that person in my home, was my dad.

When I was a young child, what made it even more difficult to understand or to make any real sense of, was that the man we knew was far different from the person he portrayed outside the protected walls of the family.

These two faces he portrayed – the public face and the face he showed us – were confounding and confusing. To those outside the family - close friends, co-workers, acquaintances - I am quite sure that he appeared to be an affable and pleasant-natured man. It would have been hard for anyone to believe that he was anything but the same guy inside the private walls of our family.

Those who knew him or knew of him had only extremely positive things to say. Over the years, as I would hear people talk about him, it was surreal and ironic to have to balance those statements with the actions that I knew inside our home.

Dad was *Dr. Jekyll and Mr. Hyde* at its worst and the only people that saw the ugliness were his family.

He tried hard to be a provider. Dad was good at what he did as a professional. He kept a roof over our heads and food on the table.

But there was a side of him that only the family saw. I remember thinking to myself as a child, *Why is he a completely different person around us than when around people from outside the family?* It confused me terribly.

He was not a regular drinker, and he wasn't a user of any kind of illicit drugs.

If his behavior was explainable in that manner and not just "Dad being who he was," it might have made more sense.

It wasn't like Dad came home, sat down in his chair, downed a bunch of beers, and then became violent. That unpredictability was the scariest and most anxiety-producing aspect of his abuse cycle. It might have been less traumatic on my family if we knew it was coming, if we had some sort of indication of a trigger, but there was nothing. We never knew what the trigger might be that would cause him to release his rage.

And honestly, he didn't need a trigger to be abusive, controlling, or manipulative.

Unfortunately, his baseline personality was that of an unpredictable and psychologically, emotionally, and physically abusive, hypersensitive man.

Sometimes, it seemed a metamorphic transformation took place in him from the likable, easygoing, mild-mannered guy outside the family to the hyper-controlling, manipulative, abusive, and rage-filled man with which we were so familiar. I swear something came over him the moment he stepped inside the door. When he came home after work, I always sensed a coldness, a callousness in his eyes.

The trigger could be something that someone said, or that supper wasn't what he wanted to eat, or his dinner was not cooked to his liking. Something as small and seemingly trivial as a laugh from Mom could bring him to violence if he thought he was being laughed at, even in fun. It took many years to comprehend this, but for some reason, he was prone to outbursts of violence over things that wouldn't and shouldn't cause a typical person to react in that manner.

The attacks were so sudden, filled with such rage and so out of nowhere that I sometimes lost temporary control of my bodily functions. Just hearing his rage-filled voice erupt caused me to lose a little control of my bladder. As a five- or six-year-old boy, I knew I wasn't supposed to wet myself and I was so embarrassed and ashamed. On some other occasions, I wanted to be brave, to try to get Dad to stop, to try to help my mom.

One afternoon, I recall playing in my room and suddenly hearing screams and a commotion coming from the basement. I opened my door and crept down the hallway, through the kitchen, and to the top of the stairs. The screams and commotion were closer now. I made my way halfway down the stairs and I could see them over by the washing machine. Dad seemed to have Mom pinned down to the top of the washer and was pummeling her. To my five- or six-year-old brain and eyes, I thought he was trying to stuff her in the washing machine. I wanted so badly to try and help, to get him to stop, but I ran back upstairs and hid out in my room, hoping that he would stop hurting my mom and that he wouldn't come get me next.

In conversations with my mother many years ago, she expressed that the violence and abuse that I witnessed as a small child was nothing new at all, that violent attacks were a fairly common occurrence, even while they were a dating couple in the early 1960s.

In several of these attacks during the time they were dating, there was a common denominator: she laughed at something that was amusing and he physically assaulted her.

There were many episodes that I am aware of that happened before they were married, but the one that really sticks out in my mind involved a pair of motorcycle riding goggles and his mother; my grandmother.

Mom told me she was at the house of my dad's family, sitting in the kitchen with his mother one day while he was out riding motorcycles with some friends. Upon his return, he walked into the house, wearing a pair of motorcycle goggles. My mother laughed at him because the goggles of the era did give a certain bug-eyed look to the person wearing them. Dad was immediately incensed by her laughter and he slapped her hard in the face. Next to being physically assaulted, the most egregious thing about this episode was that his mother was sitting right at the kitchen table to witness this! After being assaulted, Mom said she left the house for some time and went for a walk. When she returned, she was verbally accosted by my future grandmother, who said, "Don't you ever walk away from my son again!"

Why Mom ever returned to this house to be involved with these two people is beyond me.

Obviously, although I wasn't present to witness any of this, I have no reason not to believe this episode as reported many years after the fact because I witnessed this sort of behavior firsthand from my dad and my grandmother. Over the years, a much older cousin verified this and other episodes of violent abuse directed towards my mother from my dad while they were dating.

Dad's rage and temper, and propensity for

violence were well known within his family, and his mother seemed to have every excuse in the book at the ready for him. Her boy was never, ever responsible for his own misconduct. It was always something else, someone else.

Eventually, my parents would marry, but not without some manipulation in the form of direct threats from both my dad and his mother. I came along four years later.

As a small child, I remember many instances of my paternal grandmother becoming involved in domestic issues between my parents. After many violent episodes, Grandmother would often appear at our home shortly thereafter, with Grandfather in tow. The entrance was always the same, with my grandmother leading the charge, stepping inside the front door and announcing her presence. Usually, she did this with a big smile on her face. Then, in a derisive tone, she would say, "What is going on here?"

How odd and out of place my grandmother's entrance seemed. Her smirk and tone seemed incongruent to the situation.

My grandparents would come inside and take a seat on one side of the living room with their son. My mother, sister, and I sat on the other side. Soon, the accusations from my grandmother would start and they had a direct target: my mother. No matter what had happened, no matter how out of control, how dangerous, or who my dad had hurt, he was never, ever responsible in the eyes of his mother.

"What did you do, Jean?"

Or, it was "If you watched what you said, this wouldn't happen."

Or, "If you just did what he said, this wouldn't happen."

I found it odd that my grandmother was more concerned with defending her "perfect son," as she often called him, than she was about the terrible abuse to which her grandchildren were being exposed.

If Mom ever tried to stand her ground and suggested that my dad needed to accept responsibility for his behavior, my grandmother and father became further enraged at my mother for even suggesting that he was at fault for anything. It was a strange and peculiar thing to witness because it seemed that these two people nearly became one, feeding off each other's anger. And, while all this was going on, my grandfather never said a word.

Of all these incidents, one that sticks out in my mind revolves around a ride with Dad in his truck after one of his episodes, which ended in an assault on my mother. I was four or five years old and don't know what happened to cause it, but after the episode of physical violence, he grabbed me, took me outside, and tossed me inside his truck.

After I was in the truck, the next thing he did is what has always remained with me the most about this one incident. He walked to my mom's car, popped the hood, and fiddled underneath the hood. I remember sitting inside his truck, watching and wondering what he was doing.

It took many years until I figured out and understood what he was doing. He was disabling the car so Mom couldn't leave. This one action spoke to the level of outright control, vindictiveness, and lengths he would go to restrict his family.

He returned to his truck and we start driving aimlessly around town. Even though he wasn't saying much, I could sense the rage in him, so I tried to sit as far away from him as possible. When he did speak, it was in a tone and a volume that scared me. I was scared to death and just wanted to be anywhere but in that truck with him.

This was probably the first time I wished I could be somewhere else, that I could be as far away from my reality as possible. I was little and didn't like my life or the place in which I had been put. I wished I could have been a bird and flown away and not come back. But, I was a small child with no choices and no control.

After driving around and ranting, we returned to the house. Dad told me to stay in the truck while he went into the house to look for my mother and sister. A few minutes later, he stormed out, clearly enraged further, and got into the truck. He drove over to my aunt's and uncle's house, my mother's sister, who lived six blocks from our house.

Carrying her two-year-old daughter, Mom walked to her sister's house to get help. Dad and I walked to the front door. We were greeted by my uncle, who refused to let my dad in the house, but asked that he let me come in. Eventually, Dad agreed and I went inside the house.

Apparently, during the time my mom and sister had been at my aunt's home, someone telephoned my grandparents and asked that they come and get their son. Sometime later, Grandpa and Grandma showed up. As usual, my dad's mother led the charge. Even in someone else's home, my grandmother's attitude changed little. In fact, through her entrance, with the smirk on her face, the arrogance was unmistakable.

After a few minutes, they left with their son before he could hurt anyone else and they took him home. Upon their arrival home, I am sure that she fixed him his favorite meal of spaghetti and meatballs.

This seemed to be the usual Grandma solution to her son's issues. I don't know how many times I watched her fix his favorite meal after one of these episodes. In doing so, she always offered the same excuse. "My son is hypoglycemic! His hypoglycemia caused him to do this to you."

That was one of my grandmother's many excuses for his misdeeds. The cycle continued. Her son would have an episode and his parents would show up, haul him away, and keep him for a few days. He would return, and we would wait for the next episode.

It took me a while to understand the mother and son dynamic. The narcissistic mother excused the abuse of her perfect son. Her narcissistic ego was incapable of accepting her son as a human being with faults, so she blamed everyone and anything else. She never held him responsible for his actions. Her myopic view of her boy wouldn't allow that.

If it wasn't the episodes of extreme violence and out of control behavior, it was the constant and never-ending pressure of criticism, mental cruelty, and verbal abuse. The criticism and put downs of me, my mother, and sister never ended. Dad seemed to enjoy the pain he could inflict, and the more he got a reaction, the more he poured it on.

Bullying Behavior

Something as simple as giving me a name at birth was a real challenge, according to my mom. I first became aware of this over twenty-five years ago. I never really thought much of it, as it didn't surprise me.

"Your dad wanted to give you an unusual first name."

"Why?"

Mom said, "So he would have reason to laugh at and make fun of you."

As shocking as it sounds to hear, I wasn't surprised because it didn't take a strange name for my dad to make fun of or to bully me. That was what he did, and he was so good at it.

I hadn't given that conversation with my mother much thought until recently, when my maternal grandmother passed away. After the funeral service, several family members met for supper and we had a conversation about Grandma. During supper, the topic of my grandmother's name, Elaine, came up. One of my uncles turned to me and said, "Drew, your name was almost...."

I am not going to repeat the name, but it was the same name my mother had told me that my father had wanted to name me. In a way, I was shocked and astounded that I was getting validation of the conversation with my mother as the truth twenty-five years later. Not only that, but the same name too.

Five weeks prior to my birth, this same uncle had his first son. He had a conversation with my dad regarding the name that Dad wanted to give me.

"I would never give my son that name. What are you thinking?"

So, in some ironic way, I owe my uncle for not being given some strange first name.

The lack of a strange name hardly kept Dad from being a terrible bully and abuser.

One of the first incidents that I remember of being a real target of his abuse was when I was six or seven years old. I had been riding my bicycle with friends in the neighborhood, playing a game of Crash 'Em Up Derby on bicycles. It was the mid-1970s and we didn't have fancy gaming systems, the internet, or other technological toys, so we made our fun outside.

The object of Crash 'Em Up Derby was pretty simple: ram the other boys with your bicycle. At some point, someone would run into me and I'd fall off my bike.

The game was fun.

When I got home, Dad was sitting on the couch,

reading the newspaper. I was excited about the fun that I'd had with my friends and wanted to tell him about it. I told him how we were chasing each other on bikes and it turned into a game of Crash 'Em Up Derby and that one of my friends ran into me, knocking me off my bike, and it was fun!

It didn't take me long to figure out that something was wrong. The look of complete disgust, of disdain, became glaringly visible.

"You go find the boy that knocked you off your bike and you kick the shit out of him!"

That was a complete kick to the gut, a shock so complete that I didn't know how to respond. I stood there and felt my heart sink. I was shocked, saddened, and dismayed all at once. I couldn't believe what he was telling me to do.

"And if you don't, you are a worthless little chicken shit!"

I was so confused by his actions and words because I couldn't understand why he was telling me to go beat up a neighborhood boy who was my friend. I remember vividly thinking to myself, *Why would I go beat up someone I like? Why is he demanding that I do so?*

I didn't go beat up my friend. I went to my room, closed the door, and sat quietly. I wished I was a bird again. The thought of being able to fly away and not come back to this horrible environment crossed my mind. But I was a young kid with no one to turn to, nowhere to go, and no one to protect me from the awful bully.

That wasn't the end of the story.

He never forgot and the pressure from him never ceased. Over the next several days, he would return from work and seek me out.

"Did you take care of your business?"

I knew well what he was getting at.

My response to his question was always the same and I could hardly look him in the face while saying it.

"No."

Several days later, the name calling started. He stood over me with a look of disgust on his face and called me a worthless little chicken shit.

It wasn't just the words that stung so terribly or the denigrating callousness in his voice. Something else got my attention: His laugh and the snickering at me as he walked away.

It was crystal clear that he enjoyed causing pain and there was not a thing I was able to do to stop it, to make him stop. At this point, there was only one person that I thought about wanting to kick the shit out of.

I would be unable to do anything about it for many years.

Years later, I figured out what he was trying to do to me. It was obvious – he wanted to me to be a bully in his image. He wanted me to be the same vicious, violent person that he was. Since I refused to be like him, he was emasculating me and he enjoyed doing it. I didn't want to be a bully. I didn't want to be mean to anyone because I knew what it felt like to be mistreated. This went on quite often with Dad and me. He was always trying to egg me on, to instigate me into fights with other children, trying to get me to be a bully. And when I refused, he bullied me.

Every young boy wants to feel wanted, to feel accepted by his father. To be completely emasculated by that man kills the male spirit, destroys any real sense of self at a time when it is just beginning to develop.

I didn't understand the feelings that were such a huge part of my life then, but they were getting worse. As a self-defense mechanism against the bully in my house, I sank deeper into terrible anxiety, sadness, withdrawal, and isolation. It was best to be quiet and not draw any attention to myself because the large percentage of attention that I got was of the abusive type.

Sometimes, Mom asked him not to abuse any of us in the manner in which he was, but it was always best to keep quiet.

"Well, that is just too bad if you don't like it; leave if you don't like it."

Chapter 2 - No Voice, Thoughts, or Rights

Even as a young child, I knew that something was gravely wrong with my family, and I was envious of the normalcy that I saw in other families. But it wasn't until I reached my mid-twenties and started talking to professionals that I began to get a real grasp on the depth of the abuse to which we were exposed. We were abused and controlled by a very narcissistic man. His feelings, needs, wants, and voice always came first. If we didn't let that happen, we could be hurt. It was brainwashing at its worst, and he often had a partner in the constant and persistent brainwashing.

My first recollections of this sort of manipulative and controlling behavior occurred mostly in the aftermath of some explosive outburst of rage. After these episodes, the typical and recurring theme for him was to act as a mediator and a nurse to Mom if he had hurt her.

In retrospect, I find this incredibly surreal and odd, that the man who had caused the injuries played nurse to his victim.

But the most subversive thing that I remember was his talk during this time, what I call the "blaming others" phase. He made comments like "If you hadn't done this, this wouldn't have happened," or "You make me do this to you."

In essence, my mother was responsible for her own abuse and he was never, ever responsible for his actions.

The Supper Table and Dad's Feelings

Our supper table was not a place where we could enjoy a meal together, reconnect after the day, and share joy. Mostly, it was Dad's own private place, where he could abuse the entire family emotionally and verbally. During suppertime, I sat with my head down, face staring at the plate, quietly eating, anxiously and nervously waiting and wondering what he would feel the need to talk about during one of his "feeling talks."

I learned early that no one in the family – not my mother, my sister, nor I – were allowed to have feelings. Only Dad was allowed to have feelings and he expressed them often. These talk sessions could be endlessly monotonous; the only voice ever heard was his. He held us hostage to his feelings and he hijacked these family times.

The most agonizing times at the supper table were after an episode of out of control behavior and abuse. It was where Dad got to play mediator. His talk was manipulative, often completely nonsensical in terms of what actually happened to cause the latest outburst. It was impossible to get him to talk about the here and now in terms of the abuse. Talking in circles, never actually addressing the matter of his most recent episode of abuse became the norm. Like a puppet on a string, he was never responsible.

He forced us not to think about his actions in terms of him individually, but in terms of the outside world. Dad made statements like "No one is perfect in this world," or "Neither of you are perfect either; it's too bad you can't just accept me for who I am." One of the more insidious comments he would use to deflect from his behavior was "Good people are more tolerant."

I took this comment to heart for a long time. I learned to be a good victim, to tolerate abuse because I wanted to be a good person.

No Thoughts or Rights

Although my mother was clearly an adult and quite capable of making her own decisions for herself and her children, she was never treated that way by Dad. We lived right across the street from a large park, playground, and swimming pool, but she wasn't allowed to take her two small children to the park without first seeking permission from Dad. She was a stay-at-home mom, while he worked during my first few years and it was expected that she would call him at work to get permission to leave the house. Then there were the games of phone tag that he often played. While at work, he would make regular calls home to check on her and, if she didn't answer the phone quickly enough, she was given the third degree. "Where were you?" or "Why didn't you answer the phone quickly enough when I called?" More than once, he rushed home from work just to see that she was where she was supposed to be if she didn't get to the phone. Often, these types of circumstances did lead to Dad becoming belligerent and violent when he returned home in the evening. Mom could never expect to be treated as an equal, as an adult in this relationship with her husband. He didn't have a wife and two children. In his warped, narcissistic mind, he had three children that needed to be controlled and dominated in every sense. And seemingly, after every episode of abuse, we had the family sit-down sessions at the supper table moderated and controlled by him!

These mediation sessions at the kitchen table could quickly turn ugly and scary. Say the wrong thing, not listen to him like he wanted, or dare point a finger of responsibility at him, and it was amazing how fast this could re-escalate him.

You could see in his eyes and hear in his voice how angry he became when the subject of him taking responsibility for his own behavior was mentioned. The rage could be reignited if he thought our mother was demanding that he be held responsible. If the conversation swayed this way during a meal, food or dishes could end up on the kitchen floor in a split second. It was often best just to let him talk and let him blame us for his conduct rather than take the chance of further escalating a dangerous man. We had no right to demand that he not abuse us and even less rights to ask him to be responsible for his behavior. In effect, he was re-victimizing his victims.

One incident in particular speaks to the level of thought control he had over his family. After one of the many sessions at the kitchen table, Dad walked away from the table and said to us, "If you have any hurt feelings over this, you take things too personally, and that is your fault." It was normal for him to tell us exactly what our feelings and thoughts should be.

The words aren't what stick out in my mind. Instead, the crass, derisive tone and the smile on his face as he walked away, almost laughing at our pain, speaks volumes. I saw a soul devoid of real human emotion and one that enjoyed hurting others.

This taking away of rights and controlling of thoughts manifested itself in the early days of the relationship between my parents. Years later, my mom told me that she tried to break off the relationship after abusive episodes while they were dating, but she was threatened and felt railroaded into continuing the relationship. Mom said his mother got word that she was trying to end the relationship and confronted her, telling her, "You will not leave my boy! There is nothing wrong with my son!" In my grandmother's eyes, no one had any rights, no rights to make decisions for themselves, and no one had the right to say "no" to her boy.

Brainwashing

Many of our weekends and most holidays were spent at the home of my paternal grandparents. My mother came from a large family. Most of her brothers and sisters lived in the immediate area, but we rarely saw any of those families.

What we faced at the home of my grandparents was a replica of the same behavior we faced alone with my dad; only now, he had a partner in the control, manipulation, and abuse of his family: his own mother.

As I reflect on the time we spent as a family at the home of my dad's parents, it is amazing the way Dad and his mother seemed to have a symbiotic relationship, seeming to morph into one person and to feed off each other.

If a recent episode of abuse had occurred between my parents in our home, the incident was rehashed at the supper table in front of my grandparents. No one could get Dad or his mother to address the real issues behind the latest episode of violence. Mother and son were skilled manipulators, manufacturing excuses that had nothing to do with anything that caused the abuse. They manipulated the situation to deflect responsibility.

My mother tried to get them to focus on the real matter at hand, but the blame game, complete with talking in circles from both of them, made it a pointless debate. No one could ever win with these two people.

"You don't appreciate anything I (we) do for you" or "I work hard to put food on the table, a roof over your head, and this is what I get in return!"

Statements like these were always among the manipulative ways Dad and his mother deflected any responsibility for his abusive patterns.

"Everyone has problems; Joe down the street has problems."

These conversations turned into personal attacks on all of us, a diatribe about our shortcomings as human beings. If we were hurt or had hurt feelings over anything Dad or my grandmother did or said, we were told, "You take things too personally."

I remember Dad telling Mom, "If you don't like it here, take your children and go live in the street; go find out how hard life is!"

My mother could never expect to be treated as an equal in this relationship. She had no rights or voice, and she needed someone to look after her and her children. My dad and grandmother believed Mom should be happy that she got that much.

During these visits to my grandparents, it felt like Dad had three children, my mother being the third. Mother and son were there to direct Mom and her children.

All this vitriol amounted to severe brainwashing and psychological abuse. They did an effective job of it too. The lesson they pounded into our heads was that not only did we have to be responsible for our conduct, we were responsible for any abuse inflicted on us. Everything we did could be used as a tool against us to explain away any abusive episodes.

The dynamics of this mother-son relationship could become even more enmeshed if at any time my mother intimated that Dad needed "counseling." I can vividly recall the immediate rage on the faces of both of them: the skin reddening, the eyes bulging from both of their heads as they responded, "You are the one with the problems!"

Chapter 3 - A Night of Terror

This was the usual pattern in our lives until I was twelve years old. My mother filed for divorce and took my sister and me to live in California. What a culture shock that was for a quiet and distressed twelve-year-old kid from the middle of Nebraska.

A stipulation in the divorce agreement required my sister and me to spend the summer with our dad in Nebraska. On some levels, this was okay because I got to see friends and play baseball with my previous Little League team. It provided a sense of normalcy in the comfortable surroundings of my hometown.

However, it also meant we were alone with Dad. While my parents were married, it always seemed that, in a strange way, we were not only being emotionally and psychologically abused, but were also expected to provide emotional support to our father. It was role reversal and this time alone would be no different.

Revisiting the Supper Table

One evening, like he had done so many times before, Dad said it was time to talk and made us take our seats at the table. My anxiety and fear skyrocketed because I knew what these talk sessions could turn into.

"This is what family is for, to talk about things." That's what Dad said.

I didn't understand the feelings at the time, but I knew I was being used and violated by these sessions.

We were seated at the kitchen table and he took his usual seat, and it didn't take long for me to understand what this would be about. He wanted to talk about his feelings regarding the divorce. My sister and I were trapped, held hostage to his feelings of anger towards our mother. He was situated at the table in such a way that we were unable to get away from him; we had nowhere to go in any direction. At that moment, he had the opportunity to unleash all of the anger about the divorce on his two children. Almost immediately, he was enraged and out of control.

"Your mother put me through hell by divorcing me. Family never, ever leaves family!"

I felt something markedly different in his rage this time. Much more scary than any time before. It was in the tone and anger in his voice, the rage written all over his face, and mostly in his eyes. There was something frightfully menacing and dark in his eyes. Soon, Dad was out of his chair, raging about "the hell" that our mom had put him through, the financial costs of the divorce, the pain it caused him, and his need to get back at her.

In the past, we had seen him take out his frustrations by being destructive to property. This was no different. He raided the refrigerator and threw whatever he could get his hands on all over the kitchen floor.

A full carton of eggs splattered across the room. Dishes crashed on the floor.

When he turned his back to us, my sister and I ran upstairs and hid quietly in our rooms. His rage shook the house while more dishes broke on the floor.

At some moment, he must have noticed we were no longer there to view his rage because I could hear him stomping out of the kitchen towards the stairs. Hiding in my room, I could sense that he was close. From the bottom of the stairs, he screamed, "Get back down here and listen to me! Don't you make me come up there and get you!"

At that moment, as a twelve-year-old, I knew absolute fear and what it meant not to have good choices offered to me. I was terrified and confused. My mind raced between those choices. I didn't want to go downstairs to listen to him or be near him, but I also didn't want him coming upstairs to get me. I asked myself, "Do I let this enraged monster come and get me or do I go back down to the kitchen like he wants?" I just wanted it all to stop, to be able to fly away from this, like so many times before, but that was impossible.

Eventually, my sister and I did make our way out of our rooms toward the stairs. We sat down on the top step, not wanting to get any closer to the man at the bottom of the stairs. But the demand was still the same, to come down and listen.

We slowly made our way down the stairs, one step at a time. Dad directed us to the kitchen and to our seats at the table. He took his seat and told us we weren't allowed to move from these seats until he gave permission. We were barricaded, held hostage in this house with this man, with no way out and no one to rescue us.

It was like so many times before, only this time no other adult was around. My sister and I sat in our seats and cried while listening to him.

Dad then made a startling proclamation aimed at us and our mother, the person who put him through "hell." He screamed, "I am having thoughts of taking both of your lives right now to get back at your mother for divorcing me!" I didn't need him to say that; his eyes, the way he was looking at us, said as much even without him speaking those words. Because of the look in his eyes, I knew to take him seriously. Dad's threats were very serious.

Finally, after telling us how hard his life was made the previous year because of the divorce, he allowed us to leave and go to bed. He issued one more warning as we walked away.

"If either one of you tells anyone about this, I will kill both of you."

When he looked at us and made that statement, his eyes told me what was in his soul. Those eyes said everything I needed to know and understand about his threats. I took it to heart. After making the slow walk to my bedroom, I crawled under the covers and lay there, not sleeping for much of the night. For a long time thereafter, actually, many years, good sleep wasn't something I got often. That night I lay quietly in my bed, crying, and wondering at some point if Dad would be coming through my bedroom door at any moment, wanting to follow through with his threats.

I could do nothing to stop him.

For the rest of that summer, I don't think I came out of my room at night to use the bathroom, to get a drink, or anything. I was embarrassed about this for a long time, but the rest of that summer, I relieved myself in a pop can in my room at night. Every morning, I emptied the can in the bathroom.

Morning did come and I was still alive. My sister and I were alone at home while Dad had gone to work. I remember going to the telephone and thinking of making a phone call to the police or to an aunt and uncle who were living in the same town. I held the receiver in my hand, ready to dial 911 or make the call to my aunt and uncle, but Dad's threats kept racing through my mind.

He'd kill us if I told anyone and what would I have told them anyway? I had terrible difficulty expressing myself, telling anyone my feelings. How would I tell anyone what Dad had done the night before in a way they could understand?

So like always, I set my feelings to the side and tried my best to forget the terrible night before.

It's hard even to explain the dread that I felt that summer whenever Dad was around, especially at night when I was alone in my room. Although we physically survived that night, my spirit did not. What I saw in my dad's eyes and the words he spoke that night extinguished any spirit I had left.

Later that summer, he announced that we would be taking a trip to Kansas City, but I wasn't sure if that was his intention. Was this just a trip to Kansas City or did he have something else planned? What were his real thoughts?

From our home in Nebraska, it was a six- or seven-hour drive to Kansas City. Hardly a word of conversation was exchanged during this entire drive, and I remember looking at Dad driving and not liking the look on his face. It crossed my mind that we were in this vehicle with a dangerous man, a man who had previously made threats to our lives, and I never felt more vulnerable than the time in that car. Was he going to pull over somewhere along the endless countryside and kill us on some isolated prairie?

We made it to Kansas City and went to a local water park, but Dad said something to us in the parking lot that during that moment I thought was extremely strange.

"No one ever thinks of me or my feelings."

That was exactly what he wanted and needed. It really struck me how self-centered and egocentric this man was. He was a narcissistic abuser and I had to call him "Dad."

Martyrdom Status

The scariest part of his behavior, the part that caused the most fear and trepidation was reinforced during the night of terror. It was that we always had to allow him to play the role of victim, to play the martyr. Anything different put us in great danger. At the time, I didn't have a word for it, but I understood it well.

Chapter 4 – Victimology

The abuse that was part of my life taught me one thing as a child and I learned that lesson well. I became a good victim; one that quietly accepted the abuse, accepted that this was part of my life, and there wasn't anything I could do about it. Learning to be a victim and accepting victim status was a terrible badge to wear. It was ironic and tragic. On one hand, my survival mechanisms inside the home - withdrawal, isolation, quietness, depression, and repression of all emotions - may have kept me safe there to a degree, but outside of there, I seemed to be wearing a badge that screamed "victim."

The real tragedy was the damage done to my inner child's spirit, my soul, and sense of self. The constant barrage of the personal attacks on me left me with a sense of shame and self-doubt. I was no good and my dad was sure to let me know that and often. No one in this family was allowed any positive sense of self, of feeling good about life or themselves. If there was ever any hint that someone in my family felt good about themselves for any reason, he went out of his way to take it away, to tear them back down. No one other than Dad was ever allowed to feel good about themselves. Such was life with a dangerous and violent narcissist.

I was conditioned to accept abuse and not react to it because the abuser was so much bigger and stronger than I was. It was during these times, when I was being victimized by Dad verbally or emotionally, that I realized how powerless and how little control I had over what happened to me. I had been conditioned to take abuse and not react in any manner that would cause the abuser to become more dangerous and violent. At home, I had to take it. Nothing that I could do would make that person stop. What better victim than a quiet boy that doesn't respond, that just takes it?

Like any child, I had friends, but socializing was at times difficult for me, and often, I was the target of bullying by other children. I first remember this happening in kindergarten. I lived only a few blocks from school. In small-town Nebraska during the early- to mid-1970s, small children walking to and from school was normal. Over a period of time, I started to encounter the same group of older boys and they always seemed to be waiting for me. It didn't seem to matter what route I took home, they found me. It was always the same: two or three of these boys would surround me, push me around, call me names, and laugh at me. Sometimes, I wanted to respond in a physical manner, but I was scared to death of that. Not so much the act itself, but what I saw in my dad when he was out of control scared me. I knew I didn't like that feeling and didn't want to be like that. Deep down, I wanted so badly to be something different from the out-of-control person I saw at home that I stuffed my own emotions. If I let my emotions take hold and let myself go, I would have been out of control like my dad. So, I tried the best I could to ignore these boys and walk away. I also knew my odds weren't good if I tried to fight. I was one small boy, surrounded by two or three older boys.

At some point in time, my dad got wind of this problem. Instead of trying to help me find a way to deal with this matter constructively, he took the opportunity to further humiliate, embarrass, and emasculate me. Mean comments like "You really are a little chicken shit" or "You are worthless" seemed to be his normal response. Once again, I was being rejected by my dad and the best thing I could do was to hide from him, to remove myself from him. Showing hurt feelings of any sort seemed to egg him on further, causing him to laugh at and humiliate me. This man that I had to call "Dad" did not possess any sort of empathy. He was a mean, tyrannical, out-of-control bully.

To be so openly and cruelly rejected and humiliated on such a regular basis by my own father left me with deep wounds. My male ego, any positive sense of self, had been so shattered and betrayed by this horrible presence in my life that I often wished for death. I did not want my life any longer. So many times, I tried to connect in a positive way with Dad and was brushed away and rejected that it left my heart, soul, and spirit deeply scarred.

It was during these times of complete rejection that I found myself questioning life and the reason for my existence. "Why am I here?" "Why do I have to be exposed to such awful pain?" I couldn't understand why I was put in this awful situation. It would have been easy to end the pain and sadness, but I never seriously considered suicide as an alternative. In my mind, life has been a game, a marathon of sorts, and it is a game that I will win in the end. I came to the decision many years ago that I would never commit suicide because that means the people that have caused me such great pain and misery have won. I would never allow that to be the case.

After the divorce of my parents and the move to California with my mom and sister, the bullying I was subjected to seemed to intensify. Here I was, carrying around the trauma of my early life and now I was thrust into a far different place than small-town Midwestern Nebraska. I struggled terribly to find a place for me, to acclimate to my new surroundings. In Nebraska, we lived in a house outside of town with lots of open space to run around in, explore the woods, and to ride my dirt bikes in neighboring fields. In the Bay Area, though, my mom, sister, and I lived in a small apartment surrounded by other apartment complexes and lots of steel and concrete. No open fields, no trees, no place to get away from the never-ending noise and traffic of a busy metropolitan area.

Fitting in and making new friends was an extremely difficult challenge. If I wasn't getting harassed about being from a far-off place that kids were not familiar with, it was my last name, the way I looked, or the clothes that I wore. Kids could always find ways to ridicule and humiliate me. The most troublesome part was that I seemed to be ganged up on; it was never just the instigator and me. They outnumbered me with their friends to act as an audience.

It is so obvious now that I was an easy target because I had been conditioned to be one by my father. In my home, I could never respond to Dad's behavior in any way because that put me at great risk. He set me up to become a victim of other people. Being quiet and not responding emboldened those that wanted an easy victim. That first summer spent with Dad when he openly threatened my sister and me with death only served to push me further into that hole of terrible social anxiety, sadness, and withdrawal. I went back to the Bay Area after that summer, but not without lots of trepidation. It was during that second year in the Bay Area that I found myself at a real crossroads. Not only was the environment of California a challenge for me, the fact that I was living with my mom and sister presented its own obstacles. Although we were away from the abuser, we were still a family torn apart and struggling with the effects of so many years of domestic abuse and violence. I could continue to live with my mom and sister in a place and environment that wasn't for me or I could move back to Nebraska. Moving back to Nebraska meant living with my grandparents and my dad. Once again, I was presented with no good choices. I chose to move back to Nebraska because it was at least to a familiar place and surroundings.

Adult Victim

As I became a young adult, I still carried the victim badge with me. Over time, it occurred to me that this victim status is like a terrible self-fulfilling prophecy. Through my difficult childhood, it seemed that life hadn't ever been good to me, so I learned always to expect the worst, never to expect good things for myself or to have confidence that life could be good. I felt directionless and alone, and I did not have expectations that good things were meant for me or that life could be better. I was afraid. I was afraid to do anything, afraid to take chances; I lacked any real confidence. What held me back was the constant criticism, the wondering whatever I might do, positive or not, that it would be used against me by Dad and or Grandmother.

After a lot of introspection, it occurred to me that most of my fear was rooted in not only the emotional abuse, but also the manipulation by my father. Dad had this sneaky and manipulative way of stealing credit for himself for any success that I or anyone else may have had. While married to my mother, he used the word "participation" as a means to steal credit for himself. "Without my participation, you would not have accomplished that." And to him, "participation" could be something as simple as providing a roof over our head or putting food on the table. It was one more way he manipulated to gain control and keep people under his thumb.

Chapter 5 - Dad and His Mother

I remember being small and thinking to myself that not all was right in the relationship between my dad and his mother. I always had this strange sense in my gut that something was odd and I was way too young to be able to explain it. I guess at that time, the easiest and most logical explanation was that they were much too close. When they both were around, it didn't feel like what a mother-son relationship should be like.

This was especially obvious during those times when my grandmother would become involved in the episodes of abuse inflicted on my mother, sister, and me by my dad. In my grandmother's mind, neither my mother nor her children had any rights to expect to be treated fairly or with love and care by her son. If anything ever happened, she was always there to defend and make full excuses for her son and cast blame on us.

Building a Bully

When I moved back to Nebraska, it became evident, even to a fourteen-year-old, why my dad was who he was and why he behaved the way he did. He had a great teacher: his mother. As I reflect on each of their behaviors, it is amazing how much of a perfect match they were to each other.

While living with my grandparents, I was offered a first-hand glimpse of the way my grandmother controlled, manipulated, and abused her family. My grandmother even played the same game of charades that her son was so good at outside of the family. To me, this was one of the most manipulative parts of the abuse cycle because they were both offering two different faces. There was one for the outside world to see and then the ugly face they offered to their family. Many people often commented to me or other family members about how nice and pleasant and what decent people my grandparents and Dad were. I never said a word in reply to these people when they offered these kind comments, but offered a casual nod of my head. I knew something different about them.

My grandmother was in charge within the family and made sure everyone knew it. One thing that sticks out in my mind was just how mean and controlling she could be toward her husband. If she didn't get things her way, if everything wasn't just how she wanted it, and if he didn't jump when she said "jump," she would become enraged. The self-centeredness was over the top and no one dared cross her or ask her to act any differently. I think my grandfather must have just thought it best not to rock the boat and just let her do as she wished; otherwise, life around her could be hell. In real short terms, she was an emotionally and psychologically abusive bully, a child in an adult's body who threw adult-sized tantrums when things didn't go her way. It seemed that through her abuse cycle, through her manipulation and need for absolute power over everyone, she emasculated my grandfather.

My grandfather was a retired railroad worker with a nice pension. Grandmother controlled his money to the point of giving him an allowance every payday. If there were decisions to be made in the family, especially any financial decisions, my grandmother used one phrase toward my grandfather. If he had any voice in these matters, it was always met with, "Well, what do you know, you didn't even make it past the eighth grade!"

And that was true, but my grandfather was born in 1913, got sick at age thirteen, and missed a lot of school while recovering. My grandfather came from a very poor family. Instead of going back to school, he went to work, becoming a messenger for a local company. In the Pre-Depression Era, it was hardly strange for a young person to go to work at a young age to help support the family. That my grandfather never made it past the eighth grade didn't mean he was dumb; quite the contrary – it was a sign of the times and the family situation.

He often tried to have a voice in these discussions, but this did nothing more than enrage my grandmother. I saw her escalate from a casual discussion about some family issue to immediate explosive rage and anger. It was amazing how it matched exactly what her son did. The same out-of-control explosiveness, the same rage, the same manipulative and controlling ways, even the same look on her face and in her eyes. The only difference in the personality and behavior of my dad and his mother was that Dad was a physically imposing man and could be extremely dangerous, while Grandma wasn't likely to be able to hurt anyone physically.

Another conversation with my mother indicated to me just how little control he had in his own family and what he had to do to keep the peace. When I was about five years old, after a particularly violent episode with my dad, law enforcement became involved and he was put in jail. The judge gave him an option: stay in jail or go to a treatment facility.

During his stay at the treatment facility, my mother went to visit him with his mom and dad. During this visit, my grandfather pulled my mother to the side, out of sight and earshot of my grandmother, and said, "If our son is doing what you say he does to you, he has a serious problem." Then he gave my mom a hug.

I don't have to imagine what would have happened to my grandfather, how my grandmother would have reacted, if she had heard that statement. She would have gone nuts, gone absolutely ballistic and made his life a living hell if she knew he had suggested that her son had a problem.

My mother said that although my grandmother made several trips with her to the facility to see her son, she never came into the building to see him. She only sat in the car.

Years later, my mother told me that after Dad returned to the house after this period of treatment and confinement that he told her, "If you ever call the police again or suggest that I need counseling again, you will be killed."

Undermining My Grandfather

Something strange first struck me when Grandpa and Grandma would come to our house to intervene in an abusive episode in my family's home. Grandpa was always in tow, but he never said a word. Any discussions were led by Grandma and Dad, and they seemed to always be us (my mother, sister, and I) against them (Dad and his mother).

I didn't know what it meant and didn't have a way to describe what my grandmother was doing to my grandfather, but years later, it was obvious that she completely and irrevocably emasculated him as the narcissistic, controlling, and manipulative woman that she was.

In front of my grandmother, my grandfather never indicated that his son should be responsible for his actions. He never said a word in defense of the young family that his son and wife were controlling and abusing. Knowing what I do now about how my grandfather could never say anything that reflected negatively on his son's behavior, I assume this was likely the case throughout the years that Dad was growing up in their home.

My mother once told me that my grandfather made a confession to her when he learned that she was going to marry his son.

"I hope you can control him because we have never had control of him in any way."

Did he really think my mother could exercise any more control over their son than they did? At all times, Dad did what he wanted, when he wanted, and no one was going to ever tell him differently.

I imagine that if my grandfather tried to exercise any control or be a disciplinarian over his young son, his wife would have made things so difficult for him. She wasn't about to let anyone imply that her son had ever done anything wrong, not even her own husband.

Then, there was the real possibility that by the time my dad was a teen, he presented a physical threat to his own father in the event that he tried to exert some control over his son.

I witnessed my dad completely undermine his own father many times over the years, especially when I was small and there was any sort of home improvement project underway at my grandparents' home. Since we spent a good portion of our time at our grandparents' home, we were around when some project was going on: the new back deck, the new carport roof, the new air conditioning system, electrical work.

Dad was always around to "help" his father. But, more often than not, it appeared that Dad was only there to criticize, to make demeaning comments, like telling my grandfather he was doing it wrong, that Dad's way was better.

It was Grandfather's home, yet his son was hijacking these projects for himself. As I look back on it, it is clear why he thought he could treat his own father with such a lack of respect and disdain. Because that was the exact way my grandmother had treated Grandpa for decades. Dad was doing exactly what his mother always had done, and if anyone ever had a different idea than Dad did, that was when the self-aggrandizing belligerent bully showed his face.

"I don't know anything!" was a comment he used often when his ideas were met with any opposition. Statements like that really say, "Those that dare disagree with me must be stupid to not know I have the answer for everything, expert or not."

After these projects were done, we had to listen to my grandmother sing the praises of her wonderful son. I can't tell you how many times I remember her saying, "Oh, look at what my perfect son has done!" I don't think I ever heard her once say, "Thank you" or "You did a really good job on that project" to her own husband.

Chapter 6 – Taking Back Self

As I became a teenager and young adult, it was evident that to begin to heal from the terrible abuse that was much of my life, I needed to take a stand against it. For years, I tried to forget about it and move on, but some trauma runs so deep that trying to forget doesn't help. There is no forgetting. There is only a path to finding healing and recovery. Part of that recovery was understanding and coming to terms with my own feelings. For so long, I had repressed all feelings by carrying around the weight of some of the terrible trauma from my childhood experiences. Somehow, I had to become whole again, or at least as whole and healed as I could be.

Around age twenty-one, I realized I wasn't scared of my father in any way. The starting point for my healing was taking a stand against this person who caused so much pain, trauma, tribulation, and loss in my life.

There would be a time when Dad crossed the line again; there always was, and I would not back down. For some, I suppose walking away from this family and never looking back would have been a choice, but for me, that wasn't an option. If I just walked away without dealing with him, I think I would have always regretted that. Like many bullies, he seemed to enjoy inflicting as much emotional and psychological pain on me as he could.

It was vital that I be prepared for his reaction when I stood up to his abuse. Through the years, it was clear what happened when someone stood their ground with him. I had witnessed far too many rage-filled, violent episodes when someone expressed feelings he didn't like or agree with. I knew first and foremost that I had better be physically ready for whatever could happen.

Unfortunately, this meant waiting, just shoving all my feelings deep inside while waiting to get big and strong enough to do that. It was a terrible feeling, one that left me feeling lost and alone, that I couldn't hope to express my feelings openly until I could physically defend myself.

My dad and I have always been different physically. Although I do carry some resemblance to my dad in facial features, my body type is that of my mother's brothers, fairly tall and thin. Making fun of my body type was one of the ways he enjoyed emasculating me while I was growing up. He seemed to take joy in making fun of my build and pointed out many times how thin and weak I must be. Dad was a powerfully built man and, when out of control, he was mostly unstoppable. The only way to stop him was to incapacitate him in some manner.

The First Stand

In the summer of 1990, Dad lived in Utah, while I was living in the basement apartment of my grandmother's home, following the death of my grandfather one year earlier. Although we lived in different states, and had for some time, we still had fairly regular contact. He asked me to come to Utah for the summer to help him around his house. I agreed to go, as it would be my first opportunity to go back to Utah after finishing high school there a few years earlier.

During the time I was in Utah, I painted his house, worked on his backyard deck, and handled some other general maintenance issues. But I also found time to do some things other than just work around the house, like play golf and ride my new mountain bike on the trails around Salt Lake City.

One afternoon while riding my bike, I took a rather hard fall and suffered a pretty serious leg injury that left me largely disabled and unable to walk for seven to ten days. My lower left leg was swollen and had serious road rash from knee to ankle.

While recuperating from my injury, I was unable to do anything around the house and had to rest with my leg raised on the couch until the swelling went down. One afternoon, Dad was on the deck, continuing to work on the floor. For some reason, he started yelling at me about getting up off my ass. I couldn't walk or put any weight on my leg and he was out there screaming at me. It was that awful, derisive, angry tone that seemed to be the norm when talking to family members.

I simply said to him in a non-threatening manner, "Don't talk to me like that." I had experienced enough of it and wasn't going to allow him to talk to me in such a disrespectful tone. I was completely incapacitated, so I had no idea what he thought I could possibly do or how I could be of any real help.

In the blink of an eye, he rushed into the house. I could see the look on his face and in his eyes; he was coming for me like he had done so many times to my mother. I tried to stand up from the couch to defend myself, but he rushed down the stairs and was on me before I knew it. I tried to fight him off, but being hobbled and on the defensive against him, I couldn't keep him off me. I tried to defend myself, on one good leg, but he battered me and bulldogged me to the ground like he had done to my mother so many times before.

This raging man was on top of me, trying to choke me out. I don't know what caused him to stop, but he eventually took his hands away from my throat and got up. Maybe he stopped because there were a couple other people there to witness this or maybe he just came to his senses.

But it wasn't over. I thought about calling the police, but I knew from experience from when I was younger that doing that caused him to become even more violent. It took minutes, maybe more, for police to arrive and only seconds for him to hurt people.

This episode followed the same path of so many of his violent episodes from when he was married to my mother. For a period after this attack, he was incredibly enraged. He blamed me for the attack, blamed me for causing him to become violent. It was everyone's fault but his.

For a long time after this incident, I was hard on myself for letting this chance slip through my hands. I waited, knowing the time would come, that I would get a chance to get some retribution against my dad for all of the horrible stuff that he put my mother, my sister, and me through. It took a long time to forgive myself, to accept that I had no chance on that day with the injury I had against a strong and rage-filled man.

Something else struck me again that day as I thought about a response to his attack. As hard as it was for me to decide, on that day, I determined I would never make him a victim and would let someone else, a power greater than me, deal with him when that day came.

In the years after this episode I readied myself for the next time, but not to respond in a physical manner, to find the strength to walk away. I knew it meant that I couldn't react in a manner that allowed him to play the victim card. I tried the soft approach by having reasonable conversations with him and I got attacked for it. For some bullies, like my dad, the soft approach doesn't often work; it takes a more hard-edged, aggressive response.

I didn't like needing to resort to this approach because it reminded me of his behavior, but I also knew it had to be done. Over the next few years, during some instances of interaction with him, I drew a thin line, making it clear what I would and would not accept from him. I was aggressive, yet at the same time, non-physical in my response. But the message was clear and I knew he got the message I was implying: *If you ever put your hands on me in an aggressive manner again, I will do whatever it takes to defend myself.*

Sometimes I just had to turn around and walk away, leave the situation, telling myself over and over, "It isn't worth it. No matter how good it might feel to respond in a physical manner to him, it just isn't worth it." Something else helped too when I found myself just at the brink of wanting to put my fist through my dad's face. I had a good friend that I could go talk to, but that friend was also a former Golden Gloves boxer. On more than one occasion over the years, he and I put on the gloves and that helped me to let go of some of the anger towards my dad. I was often at the brink with him, but for some reason, I have always been able to take a deep breath, turn around, and walk away from him. I just knew that I wasn't going to make him a victim in the eyes of everyone else when I knew who the real victims were.

Another thought helped, too.

It isn't my job to mete out justice or punishment. I will let a higher power deal with him when that day comes for him.

I was not going to make him a victim, no matter how justified I thought it would be.

To be frank and honest, I can't describe how hard it was for me not to hit my dad in the mouth as hard as I could, to knock him silly for all of the pain and suffering and humiliation he had caused me and my family over the years. I also felt justified to a degree, but I thought it best to walk away and let it be, to let someone else deal with it.

A strange thing happened, although that took me a while to understand. I made a conscious decision to not deal with my dad in a physical manner, but a couple of times in my late 20s, I let myself get involved in physical confrontations, which was so out of the ordinary for me. After a period of self-reflection and deep introspection, one thing became clear: I was reacting in a manner as if my dad was watching, as if I was proving myself to my dad, trying to get him to accept the little boy inside of me that so badly wanted that acceptance. I finally came to the conclusion that I had nothing to prove to anyone, and certainly not my dad. The only thing I needed to do was to be true to myself and who I am.

It was truly unfortunate and unfair that I had to wait until my twenties to express my feelings, but everything I learned prior to that made it clear if he didn't like what was said, you better be ready to defend yourself physically.

After the incident in Utah, Dad wanted me to live with him, but I thought it best to put some space and distance between us, so I moved back to Nebraska. I had spent part of my junior high and high school years living with my grandparents there, so it was easy to make that transition.

Since my grandfather had recently passed away and my grandmother was still in her house and had a basement apartment, it seemed like a reasonable decision to move there. Grandmother needed help caring for her house and the yard. Living with her offered a chance for me to live cheaply. I could take a few college courses while helping her as much as possible.

Generally, I was able to deal with my grandmother and her issues. When she was having her issues, I just left her alone, sometimes for days.

I tried to have reasonable and logical conversations with her regarding what was causing her unhappiness, but a couple interactions with her indicated just how impossible this woman was to deal with.

On two different occasions, while I was having a simple discussion with her, she responded, "I am the most perfect person God ever created. I have never been wrong about anything and have never hurt anyone."

I couldn't believe the words coming from her mouth, but the real kicker was that she absolutely believed them beyond a shadow of a doubt. The look on her face and the way she said it indicated how much she believed those words.

At that moment, I realized how pointless and impossible it was to have any sort of discussion with her. It led to frustration, so it was best to leave her alone and go about my business. I needed to try to help her around the house as much as possible so I could get myself in better position to move away from her. The level of the narcissism and rage that I saw in her matched the same rage I saw in my dad, making it pointless to try to have a rational and adult discussion.

My Grandmother's Final Years

When my grandmother reached her late eighties, my dad began to spend increasingly more time at her home to help with things that needed to get done and to see that she was doing fine during the week that she spent by herself. There were times I would get a phone call from him about how infuriated he had become and how she was making things difficult on him while he was at the house.

He said, "If it isn't one thing with her, it is something else."

After a few years of spending the weekends there, my dad decided to live with Grandmother during her final years so she could remain in her own home. Although they were close, I knew what this might lead to down the road.

For the past ten years, I had been living in another city, 150 miles away. When possible, I made the drive to check in and see how things were going. During one of these visits, I was sitting in the living room, watching television. Grandma and Dad were having a conversation in the kitchen to which I wasn't paying much attention. By the tone of the conversation, they were arguing about something, but I was trying not to get involved in it. I was about to leave the house and let them deal with it on their own when I heard screams and a ruckus coming from the kitchen.

I rushed to the kitchen and saw my grandmother get up from her seat at the table and walk out onto the back patio. Dad followed quickly behind her. I couldn't believe what happened next. In a flash, Dad grabbed his elderly mother, slinging her into a corner, put his hand around her neck, and drew back his fist like he was going to punch her.

I stepped in between them, shoved my dad away, and helped her into the house. I was stunned, to say the least, but then again, I knew the possibilities with these two volatile people living together. After separating them, she began to talk about a previous violent assault inflicted upon her by her son. She said, "He had me on the floor, right here near this table, sitting on me, and nearly choked me into unconsciousness." As she said this, Dad was washing dishes; I know he heard what she told me. He did not deny what she said and said nothing in rebuttal. From the lack of a denial and the look on his face, I knew she was telling the truth.

Later, I questioned Dad and he offered, "She wasn't unconscious." I could see the lack of emotion, the lack of any empathy or compassion for anyone. No denial of assaulting his ninety-something-year-old mother, no denial of having her on the floor, no denial of being on top of her.

I told him that when I lived with her, I often became frustrated with her attitude. I also told him that I walked away and refused to engage in her self-centered, abusive, negative, and argumentative behaviors. I asked him to do the same.

"No, I will not walk away from her. I will not leave her alone."

Later during this time, Dad told his mother, "Mom, if you continue, you're going to get me put in jail."

Her response was, "I will lie to protect you."

All I could do is shake my head in disbelief. Even as a victim, she couldn't and wouldn't hold her son responsible for his own behavior.

A few months later, I got a phone call from her and could tell by the tone of her voice and the things she was telling me that she was scared. During the call, she provided more information about what caused my dad to end up on top her on the kitchen floor while nearly choking her into unconsciousness. Many years prior, my grandparents had taken out life insurance policies. These policies were for a nominal amount, but my dad found out that the policies had a clause that allowed them to be cashed out before death as long as they were paid in full. Now things were making more sense.

Grandma said, "Your dad wanted to cash the policies out to help with expenses, but I said no." After saying no, he attacked and assaulted her. Out of fear, she eventually gave in and let him cash out the policies.

She also told me that she would go to the basement apartment in her home where my dad was living to speak to him and, on an occasion or two, he physically attacked her.

"I don't know what I say that causes him to attack me."

It didn't matter; I knew it well.

"Drew, I am scared to death of him."

On more than one occasion, I suggested that she call the police, but she always said, "I will never call the police." She made it clear that no matter what he did, even as a victim herself, she would never hold him responsible.

My grandmother was pleading with me to help her. The same woman who thirty years prior had told us we were to blame for her son's behavior, that if we were better people, things like this wouldn't happen. The same woman who turned her back on the pain and suffering her son caused was now asking for help.

For a brief moment, the thought crossed my mind to ask her, "Well, didn't you keep him properly fed?" or "Grandma, what did you do to cause your son to become violent?" or "Did you feed him spaghetti and meatballs after the episode?" I thought about turning the tables on her, but I refused to do that. I knew how it made me feel when she did that to us and I knew how twisted and sick it was.

I knew the right thing to do was to keep her safe, to let her die on her own terms, but I also thought about letting her deal with it on her own. In good conscience, I just couldn't do that, so I made myself available by moving back to the area and trying to be a buffer between the two of them as much as possible. In December 2008, she passed away of natural causes in her home on her own terms at ninety-five years of age. This episode of my dad bullying and intimidating his mother to get her to cash out the policies brought to mind something else that I had always wondered about, but wasn't really sure. In the early 1990s, he spent several thousand dollars to provide his mother with an updated kitchen and replace old carpeting in her home. It certainly wasn't something that many sons wouldn't do for an aging mother to make life more comfortable. But with my dad, there always seemed to be something else at work. I never said anything, because at the time I really was unsure. Dad had the kitchen remodeled for her; putting in new kitchen cupboards and countertops, a dishwasher, and new carpet throughout the upstairs. She had lived in the same house for over fifty years and it had been paid off long ago. Then, shortly after the work was done, we learned that the house had been completely signed over to my dad, leaving his older sister out of the loop of what was going on. Now, after hearing how he got her to cash out the insurance policies, things were making more sense to me. It appeared that he had manipulated his own mother. I wondered if that manipulation included bullying, threats, and intimidation, since it appeared that that was exactly how he got the insurance policies cashed out. I don't know for sure that that was the case over the house, but it wouldn't surprise me at all. If Dad didn't get what he wanted at all times, he resorted to belligerence, then bullying and, lastly, sometimes rage-filled assaults. One of my cousins who lived nearby said that she was over visiting Grandma and Dad one day and they were having a discussion, apparently a disagreement about something. My cousin, who was fifteen years older than I was and knew my dad's behavior very well, told me that Dad was enraged and said to his mom, "I paid for the counters and cabinets and, if you don't do this, I will tear them down!" He absolutely would do that.

Chapter 7- Recovering My Spirit and Myself

For many years, before I started my healing work to recover from my trauma, there was always a question that lingered in my mind. It was a question that I wanted to ask my mother. Why didn't she run away fast from this sick family when presented with so much evidence that she should do exactly that? Why didn't she leave and not look back when she was first assaulted by my dad? If she felt trapped, or manipulated into continuing the relationship, why didn't she ask for help from her own family, a family that included five brothers? Over the years, I always asked myself, "Who in their right mind would ever continue a relationship with such people?"

As I got deeper into my healing work and in talking with therapists and mental health professionals about both my mom and dad, it started to become clear. After talking to them about her erratic behavior, after the divorce and in coming years, I was told that my mother was indicating some serious mental health issues of her own. In a sad and unfortunate sense, this offered some validation.

I went back to California to ask her these questions and many others, and her only response was, "You should thank me for getting you away from your father when you were twelve years old!" and "You made the decision to move back to Nebraska!"

During the two years I lived with my mom and sister in California, I was exhibiting all the signs of a child that needed help to recover from the early trauma of my life and she did nothing. I was struggling with sadness, social anxiety, withdrawal, ptsd, finding a place for me in our new surroundings, and she ignored this. She, in fact, made it worse and was absolute hell to live with at that time. I prepared myself for these answers and expected the exact response that I got. It became easy to walk away from her and limit contact from that time forward.

Over the next twelve to fifteen years, I had little contact with my mother until the death of her mother less than two years ago. During her mother's final days in the hospital as well as during the funeral, I saw and spoke with my mother and all seemed well. After the funeral, she returned to her home out of state and that was when things got strange. I received an email from her, thanking me for attending the funeral and also for going over to her oldest brother's home to visit with him since his children weren't close by and his wife had passed many years ago. Less than a week later, I got an email from her that was shocking, to say the least. In the email, she attacked and insulted me, telling me how embarrassed I should be, about what, I don't know, and that I never had a right to be upset with her or anything she might have done. It was at that moment that my decision fifteen years ago to have zero to little contact with her was validated. Considering the parents that I came from, the start I got in life, no matter what I did, no matter what else I accomplished in life, I had succeeded and I had won. No one would ever take that away from me.

Asking For Help

Having bottled up so many horrible memories and emotions for so long, it was scary to have to seek help. But the first time I stepped into a professional mental health setting, I was floored by the sense of relief that soon came. For the first time in my life, I was told that my feelings had merit, that any of my feelings were perfectly fine. I was getting validation of my thoughts, my emotions, my feelings and it was overwhelming. For the first time in my life, I wasn't being told how to feel or that my feelings were wrong. I never knew what that was like and it was like a tidal wave of emotions that hit me all at once. I could express myself without the threat of being emotionally, psychologically, and/or physically attacked. And I could begin to wipe the slate clean and try to find the lost soul within me that I never knew existed.

But the toughest work, the part that I continue to do on a daily basis, is the work I do on my inner child. That small child is still inside me, but now exists in an adult body. I had to somehow go back and give positive strokes, positive attention, love, and kindness to that little boy. As I started to do this, it felt strange and awkward all at once, but I understood the human psyche enough to understand the need for it. All children need to feel strong emotional connections, support, love, and kindness from their parents, but for whatever reason, my parents were incapable of that. As I began to understand the terrible dysfunction of my family, I understood my parents for the shattered and broken people that they were. Although I didn't get what I wanted and needed from them, I could still provide that for myself. In doing this for myself, I had to be able to give myself what my parents never could: unconditional love and support for me.

To do this, one of the first things I did was to tell that child inside me, "Drew, it isn't your fault." In addition, I had to relearn what it meant to really give love to myself, to have a positive self-image of me, to feel good about me when it seemed that no one else did. The most difficult part may have been talking to that little boy who was so openly rejected and humiliated by his father. I developed a sense of understanding my father for the very flawed and troubled human being that he had always been. In doing this, although still difficult, it helped me to develop some self-talk that gave the love and support that I deserved. Mostly though, I developed an attitude of "It's his problem, not mine. I am worthy of being held in high regard."

To be nearly thirty years old and just begin to understand the depth of the emotional and psychological trauma that I experienced as a child was heartbreaking. It was scary and overwhelming to know that I never was able to be the person that I was meant to be because of the trauma. The immense trauma that was much of my early life had caused me to protect myself with layers of defense, causing me to shut down, not even to know myself well, to put up walls to protect myself.

Once I started getting some help and peeling back the layers of trauma, I began to see something that even though overwhelming, was exciting. In peeling back all the layers, in facing all my fears, facing the trauma of my past, I could reshape and recondition myself. It was like a rebirth of sorts, of getting to be the person that I was always meant to be. It wasn't that I didn't like myself, but I didn't even know myself, never got a chance to be that person I was always meant to be. By recovering and healing my spirit, I was able to get a clearer picture of who I was and what was meant for me.

Part of that rebirth, though, meant that I had to mourn and grieve for the past, for what never was and never will be. I cried my eyes out for the lost little boy, the lost childhood, the loss of my spirit, the loss of joy and peace in my life that I deserved. I mourned deeply over the relationships that were destroyed, for the relationships that I sought but was never able to have, but mostly I mourned the loss of time that I would never get back.

At a point, I had a personal epiphany of sorts, something that helped me to reframe my past. Many years ago, I came up with a phrase, a little self-talk that was helpful to me in coming to terms with what happened to me. "It is what it is." And in that phrase, there is absolutely nothing I can do about it except move forward and heal myself as best as possible.

Finding Peace and Joy

There was no real peace or feelings of joy, of happiness in my life, just the terrible feelings of a family unit destroyed and lives turned upside down because of domestic abuse and violence. It has been my daily work to find something each day that brings joy, happiness, hopefulness, and most of all, peace. I find peace and joy in small things: from waking up to a beautiful sunshine-filled day, watching kids be kids, watching animals, being a part of the natural world around me. I also have to find time to laugh and smile each day. Laughter is good medicine for the soul and truly helps heal the heart. In many ways, there is still a small child in me that just wants to feel joyous, laugh, and have a good time.

I suppose that may be why I have always enjoyed being around children. I don't have any children of my own, no nieces or nephews, but I have always enjoyed any time that I could spend around children. Especially helpful were the children of a good friend. In my early twenties, when things were bad or I was depressed, I would go spend time with this family and, later, when I moved to the same larger city where they lived, I was often the person they called when they needed a babysitter for the kids. I babysat them often when they were infants and toddlers and this was especially joyful for me. I got a kick out of watching them learn about the world around them, while also playing with them and making them laugh and giggle.

Part of recovery and finding true peace and joy for myself meant that I also had to find it in me to forgive the people that hurt me, that caused me pain, and caused my life to be so disrupted. It is easy to carry resentment for things that never were, for lost time, for lost love, for lost positive relationships, but in the here and now, it does no good. In healing my spirit, trying to find the best person that I was always meant to be, I had to find forgiveness. Carrying resentment, negativity, and any of the bad stuff around steals from my positive aura. Negativity only breeds contempt and steals positive focus and energy away from me when I could use that energy for positive steps towards healing, finding peace, joy, and finding my lost spirit. It is, and probably always will be a daily journey, and that is okay. Without real forgiveness, I can't have the peace and joy that I want in my life. It isn't easy, forgiving people that caused such great pain, but I chose to work on it for one reason only. I don't do it for them; I work on forgiveness so my spirit can be more at peace. Although I may work to find forgiveness for these people, it doesn't mean that I have to forget what was done, what was taken from me, what I was deprived of or that I have to have any sort of relationship with anyone. It is a daily journey for me and one that I accepted as just part of my life long ago.

New Talent, Untapped Potential

While doing this work and uncovering the core of who I was, something exciting and new occurred to me. In finding the core of who I was supposed to be, I might uncover some untapped potential or discover a new gift. That was exciting to me and still is. I try to learn something new about myself, something positive, on a daily basis to get out of myself a bit more. Part of this rediscovery process has been about finding new talents and untapped skills and gifts.

I think everyone has untapped potential or unknown gifts, at least to them. Sometimes, it takes someone else to take notice of these gifts and talents to help us tap into that potential. Finding that untapped talent, or that unknown gift, has been extremely helpful for me and I practice it every day. Over the years, many people have told me that I had a way with the written word, with telling a story, so that is something that I work on and continue to develop over time. Writing was and always has been a very good outlet for me because it offered a safe outlet for my emotions, for being able to express myself. In addition, in doing so, it was and always has been a way for me to let things go. I think we are all given special talents or gifts that we may not be fully aware of, that we may need other people to point out to get us to maximize that potential. For me, that is what life is about: living, always learning, always growing, striving to be the best person that I can be.

New Dreams and Goals

Some of my dreams were crushed and are forever lost due to the family situation that I was put in, but it doesn't mean that I can't have new and different dreams and goals for myself. I think re-evaluating life goals and dreams is something that everyone goes through. Life throws us all curveballs and sometimes life does things to us for which we weren't ready or didn't plan. New dreams and new goals for which to strive are something that help us to create a sense of purpose. Leading a purposeful and fulfilling life is what it should be about, whether that means helping others or helping yourself to some degree. Meeting new goals and fulfilling new dreams breeds a new confidence, new love for self that is good for everyone.

Getting Out Of Victim Status

Without goals, without something to work towards, no matter how small they may seem, life can be overwhelming. It is amazing how meeting just a few small goals can enlighten the spirit, can make you feel human like life is worth living. Crossing off a goal and finding a new one to aim towards creates a newfound sense of self-worth, of confidence, of feeling better about whatever circumstance may have been placed in front of me.

The goals can be anything: educational, vocational, getting a new job, learning a new skill, taking up a new hobby, or stepping outside your comfort zone. For me, educating myself was and always will be important. I believe in lifelong education, always to be learning something new. And that doesn't have to mean taking classes. It can be reading a new book, learning to play an instrument, starting a new hobby, but number one on my list was finishing a college degree and I did that. It took me a while, but that was okay. I finished and I will continue to educate myself. Life is supposed to be about learning, growing, and making the most of the time we have.

New Sense of Self

For me, one way I have developed a more positive self-image and sense of love for self is by treating myself well. As part of my healing process for my mind, body, and spirit, I think it is vitally important to take care of my physical being and health. Watching what goes into my body, getting exercise, staying active, and interacting with the environment around me leads to more positive feelings of self. It is amazing, and sort of a self-fulfilling prophecy that by treating our bodies well from the inside out, we learn to feel good about and have a more positive self-image. This doesn't mean I still don't indulge in a sports bar hamburger now and then, because I do allow that. I just really pay attention to what goes into my body. I just make sure to balance it with a good diet and by keeping an active lifestyle.

Over the years, many mental health professionals have said, "I am shocked that you have never had any substance abuse issues." My only answer is related to the above, of treating my body well and not feeling compelled to mask my feelings. I wanted to know my feelings, to understand them even in the deepest and scariest places. I couldn't really know myself or my feelings if I did that to my body. I also had dreams as a child of being a professional baseball player and I knew that putting illicit drugs in my body wasn't the right thing to be doing. To feed my love for the game of baseball, I have continued to play the game as an adult and have also been involved in coaching Little League teams. Giving back to kids is something that has also helped me with the healing process.

Along with eating right has been getting regular exercise. Staying active is not only good for the body, but it is good for the mind. Getting the blood pumping and increasing endorphins to the brain can help to alleviate symptoms of anxiety and depression naturally without the aid of prescription medications. The real difference-maker, though, that couldn't happen without treating my body well and getting regular exercise has been retraining and relearning how to sleep. I really believe that through proper diet, treating myself well, and getting regular exercise, my body is now in its best possible position to heal itself at night with good sleep. I am most thankful for that, because when I am properly rested after a solid night of sleep, I can see a huge difference in my mood and outlook. When properly rested, I am far less stressed, feel far less anxiety, and I generally have a bright outlook.

In the end, by accepting my life as it is and just "letting it be," I came to the conclusion that I have a choice and have good options. That choice, those options are to be bitter and unhappy or to move forward and be happy. I know what I choose.

For more information on domestic abuse and violence, mental health, co-dependency, trauma reduction and other issues please visit the websites below.

www.mentalhealthamerica.net

www.nami.org

www.ncadv.org

www.domesticabuseproject.com

www.apa.org

www.narcissisticabuse.com

Printed in Great Britain
by Amazon